CW01019484

SUPERBASE 5
MILDENHALL

SUPERBASE 5

MILDENHALL

Multi-mission Task Force

David Davies and Mike Vines

Published in 1989 by Osprey Publishing
Limited
59 Grosvenor Street, London W1X 9DA

© David Davies 1989

This book is copyrighted under the
Berne Convention. All rights reserved.
Apart from any fair dealing for the
purpose of private study, research,
criticism or review, as permitted under
the Copyright Act, 1956, no part of this
publication may be reproduced, stored
in a retrieval system, or transmitted in
any form or by any means, electronic,
electrical, chemical, mechanical, optical,
photocopying, recording or otherwise,
without prior written permission. All
enquiries should be addressed to the
Publishers.

British Library Cataloguing in Publication
Data

Davies, David, 1943–
    Mildenhall
    1. Great Britain. Royal Air Force.
    Aerodromes. Mildenhall RAF Station, to
    1988
    I. Title
    358.4′17′0942643

ISBN 0-85045-894-3

Editor Dennis Baldry
Designed by David Tarbutt
Printed in Hong Kong

Front cover Those large engine
nacelle pods identify Stratotanker
Virginia Dare as a re-engined
CFM56-powered KC-135R. The US
Air Force is currently about half-
way through funding the conversion
of some 732 J57-powered KC-
135A/Qs to KC-135R configuration

Back cover Mildenhall's hangars
were obviously not designed with
the future products of Boeing
Military Airplanes in mind—this 10th
ACCS EC-135H has to hang its tail
out in the breeze

Right This handsome 'welcome
board' mural graces the Military
Airlift Command Terminal at
Mildenhall, which was opened in
1973, and is the first sight many US
servicemen and their families get of
the United Kingdom

Title pages A 60th Military Airlift
Wing Lockheed C-141B Starlifter,
better known in this European One
camouflage scheme as a 'Star
Lizard', lines up on RAF
Mildenhall's 11,000 foot runway to
fly back home to Travis AFB,
California

For Annette and Frances

Introduction

Royal Air Force Mildenhall is located in Suffolk near the English university city of Cambridge. When newly-opened, the airfield earned its place in the annals of aviation history as the starting point of the MacRobertson Air Race from England to Australia in October 1934. The winning aircraft, a de Havilland DH.88 Comet named *Grosvenor House*, arrived in Melbourne after completing 11,300 miles in less than 72 hours. Fittingly, over half a century later, that same aircraft returned to display at Mildenhall's Air Fete '87 following a remarkable 14-year restoration to flying condition.

During World War 2, RAF Mildenhall played a key role in the bomber offensive against Nazi Germany. In more than 8000 sorties, Bomber Command aircraft based at Mildenhall dropped nearly 28,000 tons of bombs on the enemy. When hostilities ended, Mildenhall was downgraded to 'caretaker' status, but returned to active service when the Cold War began to freeze solid in the wake of the Soviet Union's Berlin Blockade of June 1948. At the invitation of Clement Attlee's Labour Government, American airpower was deployed 'over there' again in strength to bolster the defences of Western Europe. Mildenhall became one of several former RAF airfields to be 'taken over' by the US Air Force.

Today, RAF Mildenhall is home for approximately 3389 military personnel with 185 US and 269 British civilians employed. The only host unit at Mildenhall (as distinct from numerous tanker/transport units deployed there on a temporary duty (TDY) basis) is the 513th Airborne Command and Control Wing, which operates the Boeing EC-135H (pages 33–58).

For the cluster of dedicated aviation enthusiasts at 'spy corner'—the car park and public viewing area on the north-east corner of the airfield—the most eagerly awaited event at Mildenhall is the launch of an SR-71 mission. But the huge variety of other aircraft movements at the base is reason enough to spend all day there with binoculars, radio and notebook (not forgetting sandwiches and thermos) to hand.

SUPERBASE 5: MILDENHALL was shot between April and June 1988 using Pentax 6 × 7 cms and Nikon 35 mm cameras loaded with Fuji film. This book would not have been possible without the generous assistance of Captain Ruthellen Lethbridge-Borden, Chief of Public Affairs, and the ever-helpful Jeff Halik. David Davies and Mike Vines would also like to thank Brian Barfoot of Leeds Camera Centre in Birmingham; Mark Reynolds of Fuji (UK) Ltd; and John Azzmat, Brian Quirke and Dave White of ICL Ltd, Birmingham.

Oshkosh, by gosh. Said to be the world's largest fire engine, the 513th Civil Engineering Squadron, Mildenhall Fire Department's Oshkosh P-15 can pump 1200 US gallons of water or 90 gallons of foam per minute from its roof-mounted foam gun

Contents

Det 4 and the SR-71

SR-71A 64-17980 of Detachment 4, 9th Strategic Reconnaissance Wing blasts off from Mildenhall as dusk falls, riding the 65,000 lb st combined thrust of its two Pratt & Whitney J58 engines. Acceleration is such that gear limiting speed comes up *very* fast. 'You just hang in there on take-off, one hand on the pole, the other on the gear select, to get the wheels up before you exceed the 300 knots limit,' says 17980's pilot Major Duane Knoll. Within a couple of minutes of lift-off he was overhead Mildenhall at 18,000 feet, turning on track to rendezvous at FL260 off England's East Coast with a KC-135Q tanker for the thirsty SR-71A's first 'top-up' of its unique JP-7 fuel. Note for lovers of trivia: so fast is the SR-71A that if a rifle bullet was fired at the moment it lifted off on an around the world flight and the bullet could maintain velocity, the Blackbird would get home 30 minutes ahead of the slug. . .

Back in the barn, 64-17980 undergoes engine servicing. The variable position inlet spike from the port J58 has been removed and can be seen on its stand to the right of picture behind the steps. Two equipment bay access panels are open. In these compartments combinations of close-look cameras, Sideways Looking Airborne Radar (SLAR) and Electronic Intelligence (ELINT) recording devices are carried on operational missions. Det 4 comprises some ten officers, 80 enlisted servicemen, 50 civilian technicians, and two flight crews who man the unit on a 45-day temporary duty (TDY) basis. The 9th SRW's permanent 'home' is Beale AFB, California

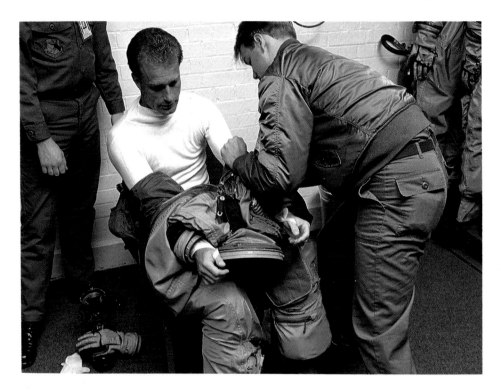

Above left and right Det 4 pilot Major Duane Noll, dressed in his 'skivvies', is helped into his David Clark S1030 'gold' pressure suit about an hour before scheduled mission time. The S1030 was developed from the suits worn by astronauts on the Gemini programme, weighs 45 pounds and costs $30,000. 'Suiting up' for an SR-71A mission takes about 12 minutes, and includes full suit pressurization and oxygen tests. And in case you wondered, yes, in-flight 'relief' is possible when wearing the S1030, but at a price. Not so much spending a penny as a hundred bucks, because that's what its costs the USAF each time a Blackbird driver goes to the john in his SR-71: the suit's integral plastic relief tube and urine bag have to be thrown away after use and new ones stitched in

Lower left Reconnaissance Systems Operator (RSO) Major Tom Veltri checks the rubber inner of his GN-121394-03 helmet for oxygen leaks

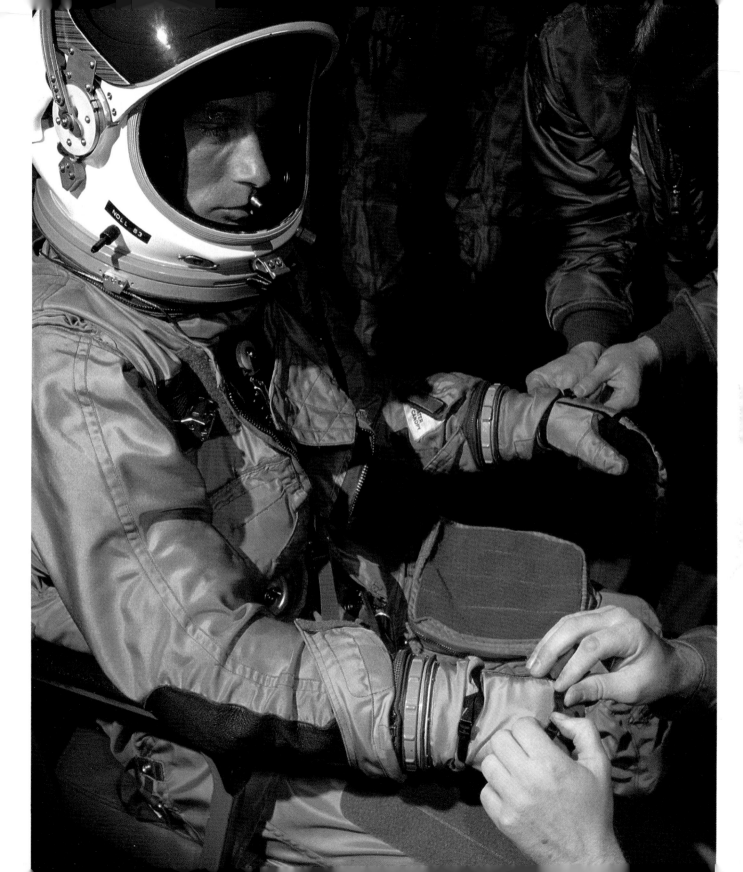

Above Pilot Major Duane Noll (left) and his RSO Major Tom Veltri are driven from the PSD fitting room to the Det 4 'barn' in a PSD van which is fitted with fully reclining 'space couches' and an inbuilt pressure suit ventilation system to keep the crew cool en route to the aircraft, which can just be seen through the van's rear doors

Right Looking not unlike a scene from an early space exploration mission, Major Tom Veltri (left) toes the red line over which ordinary mortals fear to cross because of the lurking armed guard. Veltri and Noll have just emerged from the PSD wagon and are about to strap in for a short two-hour mission. Printed patches on suit cuffs are emergency ditching checklists

Like a snake charmer a Det 4 crew chief coaxes 'Habu' 64-17971 out of its lair, while groundcrew conduct 'last chance' visual preflight checks on the hammerhead before the Blackbird lines up on Mildenhall's Runway 11 for take-off

Nosewheel precisely on the runway centreline, mainwheels still chocked, 64-17971, callsign QUID 76, awaits the 'go' signal light from the backup aircrew in the control vehicle, who monitor preflight engine run-ups and get the green light from operations director QUID 54 in Mildenhall's control tower. Like all SR-71A operational flights, QUID 76's mission today will be conducted in total radio silence. A coded message alerts relevant air traffic control units prior to each mission

Right on the button of scheduled departure time at 1000 hours QUID 76 lifts off at around 230 knots. With only 50 or 60 per cent of maximum fuel load aboard—a safety margin which provides a greater level of asymmetric flight control should one of the J58s fail on take-off—Noll and Veltri will be doing 300 knots as they pass the airfield boundary. Those diamond-studded 'tiger tail' afterburner shock waves are about 25 feet long

Home again. Coming over the fence at about 155 knots, nose pitched up at 12½ degrees, the returning QUID 76 looks almost benign after the raucous brutality of its departure

Main picture The 40-foot diameter bright orange drag chute slows the SR-71A rapidly as it rolls past the 8000-foot remaining marker on Runway 29. To the right of the picture is the small drogue which extracts the main chute from its housing on the SR-71's dorsal 'boat tail' fairing

Above Blackbird Boss. Lieutenant Colonel Nevin Cunningham, Commander of Det 4, 9th SRW at Mildenhall, has two SR-71As and two full crews under his command. Apart from occasional air tests following maintenance, all missions flown from Mildenhall are operational strategic reconnaissance sorties. Cunningham, operating as QUID 73 from his command vehicle for this mission, says the USAF have now cleared the SR-71 for operation by female flight crews

Left How's this for a cherished licence plate?

Above Cunningham shepherds QUID 76 back to its open ended barn

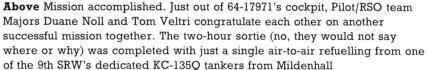

Above Mission accomplished. Just out of 64-17971's cockpit, Pilot/RSO team Majors Duane Noll and Tom Veltri congratulate each other on another successful mission together. The two-hour sortie (no, they would not say where or why) was completed with just a single air-to-air refuelling from one of the 9th SRW's dedicated KC-135Q tankers from Mildenhall

Right Once back in the barn Lockheed and Pratt & Whitney civilian technicians—some of them with experience dating back over 25 years to Kelly Johnson's Skunk Works design team—swarm over the still-hot SR-71A like bears round a honey pot, replacing safety pins and placing fans near the mainwheel units to cool the brakes. In high speed cruise the Blackbird's exterior heats up to around 600° Celsuis, and during long missions crews warm up their 'boil in the bag' liquid snacks by placing them alongside the cockpit windows

The annual Air Fete held at Mildenhall each spring provides Det 4 with a rare chance to show its public face. Here Major Duane Noll signs autographs at Air Fete '88 in front of one of the unit's two SR-71s, while crowds cluster round Det 4's sales booth, invariably the best patronized on the base. 'The public just want to be part of it all' said one very proud member of the 'Skunk Works Souvenirs' stand, where demand for stickers, patches, coffee mugs, baseball caps, T-shirts and stick-pins runs hotter than a Blackbird's skin, but the *Bud's* always good and cold

Left and above Gas stations. Blackbirds drink a special brew of fuel known as JP-7, and need special tankers to deliver it. The 349th and 350th Air Refuelling Squadrons are dedicated SR-71 tanker units forming an integral part of the 9th Strategic Reconnaissance Wing. Wherever the SR-71s go, you'll also find their distinctive four Maltese Cross on yellow band-bedecked Boeing KC-135Qs, seen here on the Mildenhall ramp close by the SR-71 barns. On a typical mission three or four KC-135Qs are launched in advance to be on station well before the allotted rendezvous time. JP-7 is a high flashpoint fuel which provides protection from possible explosion due to high airframe and fuel temperatures in high speed flight. It is said that you could throw a lighted match into a pool of JP-7 on the hangar floor and it would not ignite. We'll take their word for it

Below *Star Cruiser*, KC-135Q 59-1468, pictured during an evening of ground runs of its noisy non-fan J57 engines. Although the 'Qs are dedicated to refuelling SR-71s with JP-7, the tanks can be purged on the ground and 'regular' jet fuel loaded to service other USAF and NATO aircraft

Mission support. Three KC-135Q GLOBs (Ground Loving Old Bastards) launching from Mildenhall at sunset on 25 April 1988 in support of a reconnaissance sortie by SR-71A 64-17980. No need to ask why the noisy, smoke-trailing J57-engined KC-135 variants are not exactly flavour of the month with environmentalists. Take-off thrust is boosted by water/alcohol injection into the engine combustion chambers. Other KC-135 variants are undergoing a continuing engine retrofit programme with Pratt & Whitney JT3D-3B and CFM International F108-CF-100 (CFM56-2B-1) turbofans replacing the J57s, but to Suffolk residents the sight (and long lingering sound) of 'smoky joe' KC-135Qs climbing out of Mildenhall still signals an imminent Blackbird launch. On this mission the first tanker took off one hour and forty minutes before the SR-71A, the last just half an hour ahead

10th ACCS: EC-135

Left Under the (American) Eagle eye of the unit's mural, Major Rich Henry and Captain Dan Reilly of the 10th Airborne Command and Control Squadron check their 'game plan' for an EC-135H mission. The mural was painted by 10th ACCS Airman Rick Shad

Above Commander of the 10th ACCS Lieutenant Colonel Rich Stammler at the controls of EC-135H 61-0285 *Silver Dollar*. The 10th ACCS is part of the Mildenhall's host unit, the 513th Airborne Command and Control Wing. The EC-135s are fitted with extensive communications equipment for their role as survivable strategic emergency airborne command and control posts supporting commanders-in-chief, in the 10th ACCS's case the US Commander in Chief, Europe (USCINCEUR) and the Supreme Allied Commander, Europe (SACEUR). The Mildenhall-based EC-135H's secondary mission is to provide emergency airborne refuelling facilities for USAFE aircraft

You don't cross that rope without permission in this sensitive and secure area. Even groundcrew working on the EC-135 aircraft have to show their passes each time they cross the line. Inside the EC-135's tightly packed fuselage are crew stations for the Communications and Battle sections and a rest area. Typical crew complement comprises a flight crew of four, a general officer and up to 18 systems specialists

WARNING

Restricted Area

It is unlawful to enter this area without
permission of the Installation Commander.
Sec. 21, Internal Security Act of 1950,50 U.S.C. 797

While on this Installation all personnel and
the property under their control are subject
to search.

Left and below *Silver Dollar*, proudly bearing the inscription 'First National Emergency Airborne Command Post 1962' painted on Stateside when it returned home for a visit, and *Dark Angel* (61-0286) are among four EC-135Hs operated by the 10th ACCS at Mildenhall, all of which are undergoing a $400 million communications upgrade, scheduled for completion by 1990

Right EC-135H 61-0291 wears the crests of the 10th ACCS, USAFE and the Silk Purse Control Group which is part of the worldwide airborne command post system and is staffed by 58 personnel from all four US military services. Five battle staff teams, each composed of nine joint service personnel, perform alert and other mission functions

Aircraft captain Major Mike Lauro and copilot Major Bruce Monk take EC-135H callsign AXE 10 up into the blue at 28,000 feet and 270 knots after taking off from Mildenhall with 120,000 pounds of gas aboard (note complex fuel system schematic, switchgear and tank contents gauges above power levers to left of Monk's knee). The EC-135H's four Pratt & Whitney TF33-PW102 (JT3D) turbofans burn about 12,000 pounds of fuel per hour

AXE 10's flight navigator Captain
Mike Zimmerman at work plotting
the EC-135's course en route to
Track 7, an air refuelling area which
stretches from Yeovilton to Land's
End in the far south west of England
where it will rendezvous with
another 10th ACCS aircraft

AXE 10's flight crew (left to right):
Captain Mike Zimmerman
(Navigator); Major Mike Lauro
(Pilot); Major Bruce Monk; (Co-
pilot); Captain Charlie Stephens
(supernumerary pilot); Master
Sergeant Paul Steahl (Boomer)

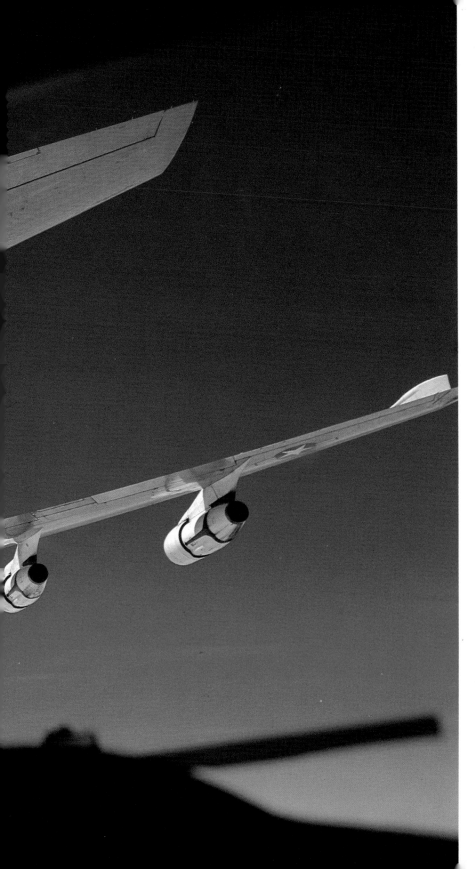

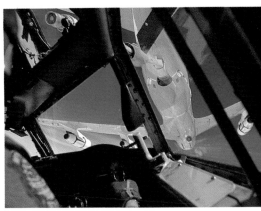

Above and overleaf *Steady, steady!* Almost there as the boom nozzle clears the cockpit on its way to the refuelling receptacle above and behind the receiver's flight deck and . . . *Made it!* The flight deck windows fill with wing as the two EC-135s fly joined together by the boom. Each 10th ACCS pilot must log 15 minutes of 'link-up' time every 45 days to maintain operational proficiency. These crews spent 90 minutes making and breaking contact, giving . . .

Left Companion EC-135H, call sign AXE 22, holds steady as Mike Lauro slides AXE 10 into position for the link up. The funnel-shaped orange drogue beneath the tanker aircraft's fuselage helps deploy a five-mile long copper coated trailing wire VLF communications antenna, enabling contact to be made with deeply submerged submarines. What length of aerial is usually deployed? 'Well, that would give away the frequency, wouldn't it?', a systems operator replied diplomatically

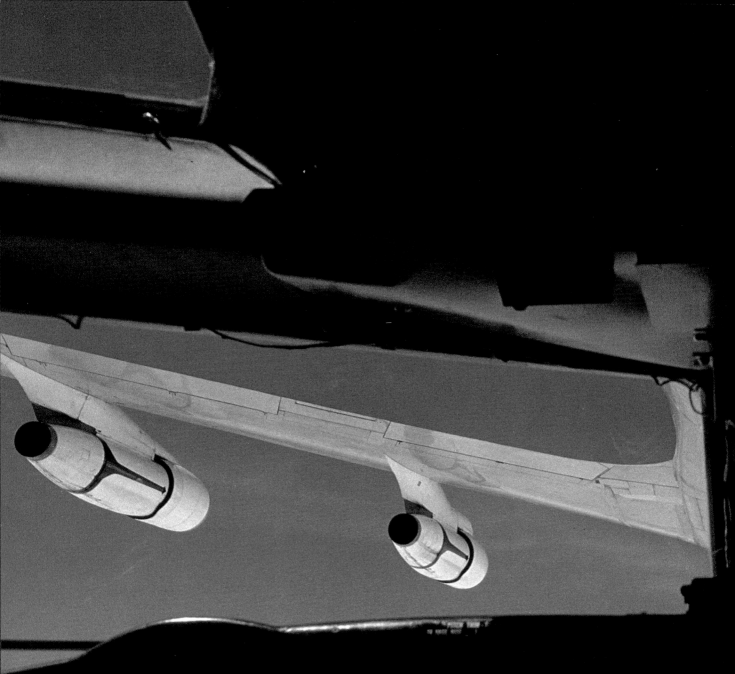

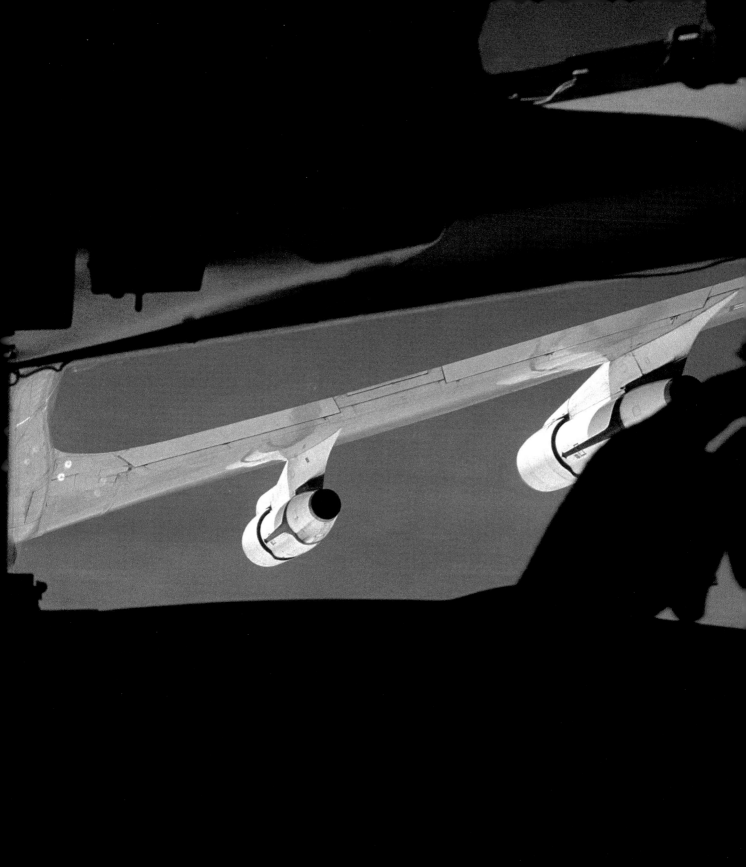

. . . receiving: AXE 22 'plugged in' to AXE 10's boom

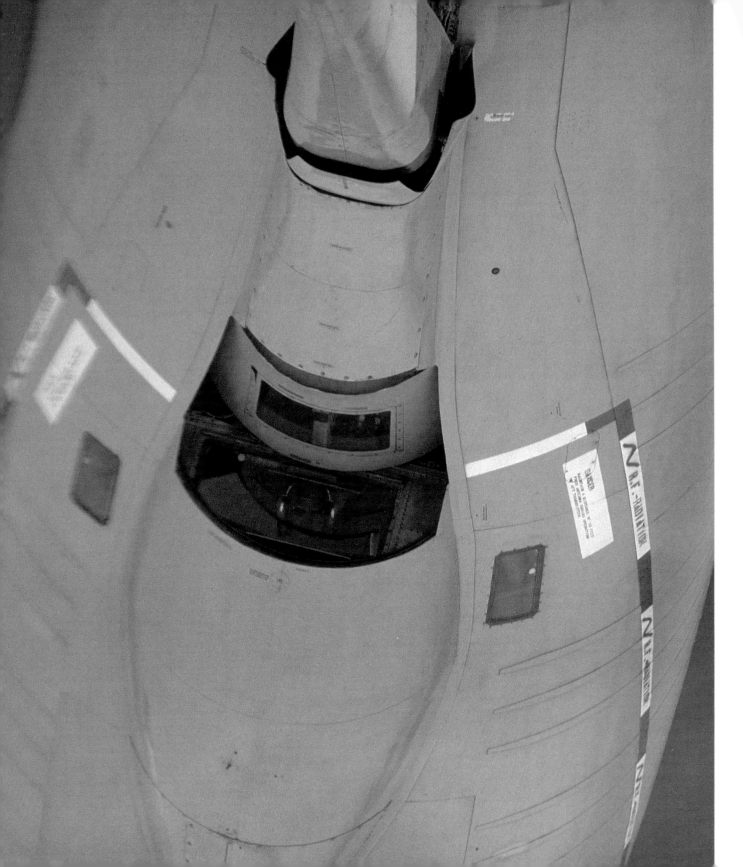

Left The only crewman (literally) lying down on the job is the boom operator. Here AXE 22's Boomer can be seen looking down from his station, stretched prone on a mattress with a chin support while he 'flies' the EC-135H's boom into the receiver aircraft's refuelling receptacle

Right AXE 10's Boomer, Master Sergeant Paul Steahl, flies the boom over the heads of AXE 22's pilots as they practise link-ups

Overleaf EAGLE FLIGHT 512, 513, 514 and 515—four McDonnell Douglas F-15C Eagles from the USAFE's 36th Tactical Fighter Wing out of Bitburg, West Germany—form up at the rear of EC-135H AXE 10 after suckling 4000 pounds of fuel apiece in complete radio silence on the Track 6 refuelling area over the North Sea. To service F-15s the EC-135 must maintain a steady 315 knots

Preceding page and these pages
Seven hours after take-off home plate comes back into view as AXE 10 returns from the West to shoot mission end practice approaches on Mildenhall's 11,000 ft Runway 11

Overleaf Ever alert: guarded and floodlit the appropriately named *Dark Angel* stands ready for duty on the 10th ACCS ramp

RC-135s

Left Warts'n'all. The Boeing RC-135U is a specialist electronic reconnaissance/signals and communications intelligence gathering variant of the C-135 family, operated by the 55th Strategic Reconnaissance Wing from Offutt AFB, Nebraska on detachment to the 306th Strategic Wing of the Eighth Air Force at RAF Mildenhall. Aircrews are provided by the 38th Strategic Reconnaissance Squadron, mission electronics specialists by the 343rd SRS. Three RC-135Us were converted from earlier RC-135C models. This is 64-14849, named by its crew *Bark like a Dawg*. Note 'chin' sensor housing and slab-sided fuselage fairing for Sideways Looking Airborne Radar (SLAR)

Right If you're wise you don't argue with a 513th Security Police Squadron guard carrying a Colt 5.56mm M-16 automatic rifle! Security around the RC-135 dispersal at Mildenhall is as sensitive as in the SR-71 barn area. To get these pictures special permission had to be granted by Strategic Air Command Headquarters in Washington, DC, and the confirmatory telex shown to rightly suspicious guards by a member of the 306th Strategic Wing as well as to our guide Geoff Halik from Mildenhall's Office of Public Affairs

Bark like a Dawg is festooned with sensors including blade, dipole and blister antennae, chin and ventral radomes, SLAR 'cheeks', extended tailcone and ventral camera pack in the position occupied by the refuelling boom housing on KC-135s

Left and far left As many as ten separate reconnaissance/ELINT versions of the C-135 have been identified, each differing in the combinations of sensors and equipment installed, which may even be unique to individual aircraft within each sub-type. 64-14844 is an RC-135V named *Anytime Baby*, one of seven converted from RC-135Cs. Ground air conditioners are used to keep sensitive electronic equipment cool

Below *Wild Thing* is an RC-135W 62-4134, having previously been an RC-135B and RC-135M. The role of the Pink Panther in electronic snooping is unclear . . .

Left *Wild Thing*'s crew embarking for a flight to Greece, where RC-135s are regularly detached to Hellenikon AB at Athens Airport. These information gathering aircraft often carry as many as 20 signals specialists and linguists from the Electronic Security Command to monitor and interpret electronic, signals, communication and telemetry data from Warsaw Pact sources, including surveillance of the Soviet air defence system and missile and space programmes. With in-flight refuelling the RC-135s have a mission endurance of 12 hours or longer

Overleaf Another RC-135W, 62-4139 *Bet On It*, seen being overlooked from the purpose-built guard post near Mildenhall's RC-135 ramp, and returning home after a long mission. Noteworthy is the long 'thimble' radome, wingtip HF probe and forest of ventral blade aerials. Count 'em. While the precise role of RC-135s is highly classified, their mission is succinctly summed up by a patch worn by a member of the 306th SW: *In God we trust, the rest we monitor*

European Tanker Task Force: KC-135A/135E and KC-10A

Above First flown in August 1956 the Boeing KC-135 Stratotanker remains the mainstay of Strategic Air Command's air refuelling force with some 594 still operational in early 1988, many upgraded in three modification programmes to enhance the aircraft's capability and extend its operational life beyond the year 2020. 56-3642 is an original KC-135A variant powered by four 13,750 lb st Pratt & Whitney J57-P-59W engines and operated by the 92nd Bomb Wing based at Fairchild AFB, Washington State. The 'Seattle Sea Hawks' logo on nose and fin tip is from the famous American Football team

Right 59-1522 *Haulin Ethyl* has her drogue 'basket' removed from the High Speed Boom by her crew chief and men of the 513th Field Maintainance Squadron based at Mildenhall. Total fuel capacity of the KC-135A is 31,200 US gallons

contained in integral wing tanks and below-floor bladder cells. The telescopic air refuelling boom comes in standard (limited to 330 knots maximum) and high speed versions, delivering about 900 US gallons per minute. Inverted V-shaped 'ruddervator' control surfaces visible in the picture enable the boom operator to 'fly' the boom to the receiver aircraft's AR receptacle via a miniature joystick control

Appropriately named KC-135A
Haulin Ethyl from the 410th BW at KI
Sawyer AFB, Michigan newly
arrived among the Mildenhall
buttercups for six weeks TDY

Main picture and above We're from Texas. How'd y'all guess? *Iron Butterfly*, KC-135A 63-8876 displays a map of the Lone Star State and an a good ol' longhorn on its fin tip.

Above and right KC-135E nose art—what better name for a tanker than *Gas Passer*?

Four KC-135Es of the 452nd Air Refuelling Wing, AFRES from March AFB, California doing a spell of TDY at Mildenhall. Left to right: 57-2603 *Baby Doll*, 56-3623 *Silver Bullet*, 58-0053 *Gas Passer* and in camouflage the un-named 57-1512. Since 1981 some 134 KC-135As serving with Air National Guard and AFRES units have been upgraded to KC-135E standard by the replacement of their J57 jet engines with Pratt & Whitney JTD-3B turbofans salvaged from Boeing 707 and 720 commercial transports. The turbofans provide a 30% increase in thrust, 14% lower fuel burn and up to 90% reductions in noise and smoke emissions. The USAF estimates that the re-engining programme will save eight million gallons of fuel per year. Compared with the KC-135A, the -E is able to offload 37% more fuel over a 2500 nautical mile operational radius

These pages The crew of KC-135E 57-2603 *Baby Doll* await the start engines signal as a KC-135R of the *Black Knights* 19th Air Refuelling Wing from Robbins AFB, Georgia crosses the threshold. The KC-135R is the latest KC-135 variant, developed by Boeing Military Airplanes to improve fuel economy and reduce noise. The KC-135R is powered by four 22,000 lb st CFM International F108-CF-100 (CFM56-2B-1) turbofans and is readily identifiable by its large engine nacelle pods. Electrical, hydraulic, fuel management and flight control system modifications are also incorporated, the main landing gear strengthened to cope with increased gross weight limits, and dual APUs installed for rapid engine starting. First re-deliveries of KC-135Rs were made to SAC in July 1984, with more than 100 currently on strength

Overleaf Cheerful Suffolk daisies relieve the dreary low-visibility camouflage of this 452nd AREFW KC-135E, a stark contrast to the more familiar shiny grey *Corogard* finish of the tankers. As yet no popular name seems to have been given to this drab scheme, which is decidely *un*popular with the army of aircraft enthusiasts who watch over Mildenhall activities from its perimeter fences

Above KC-135E on TDY from the 452nd AREFW, March AFB, California

Left Camouflaged KC-135R *Virginia Dare* of the 19th ARW has low-visibility fintip markings instead of the *Black Knights* usual black and yellow chequerboard panel

Below Airman First Class Jeff Kaminski from New Jersey has only been in the Air Force 18 months, but he's having a ball on his 45-day TDY at Mildenhall with the 19th ARW's Organisational Maintenance Squadron. Just back from a few days at RAF Leuchars in Scotland, Jeff is pictured at the controls of KC-135R *Virginia Dare*

Golden afterglow highlights the contours of a camouflaged McDonnell Douglas KC-10A Extender of the 68th AREFW from Seymour-Johnson AFB, North Carolina

SAC has to be able to deliver fuel at any time of the day or night, hence the nocturnal activity of this European One camouflaged KC-10A Extender, complete with armed guard

In SAC's high-visibility scheme is KC-10A 79-1710 of the 2nd BW from Barksdale AFB, Louisiana. Delivery of the last of 59 KC-10As to the USAF was made in late 1988. Based on the commercial DC-10-30CF, the Extender can carry a total of 356,065 pounds of fuel and is equipped with both an advanced aerial refuelling boom permitting a delivery rate of 1500 US gallons per minute, and a hose-and-drogue system enabling it to refuel US Navy and NATO aircraft. The KC-10A can also accommodate up to 169,409 pounds of cargo; on overseas deployments of fighter aircraft it is able to 'tanker' them and carry their support equipment

'Bravo Squadron': C-130E

The 'Green Hornets' from 61st Tactical Airlift Squadron, 314th Tactical Airlift Wing, Military Airlift Command out of Little Rock AFB, Arkansas brought 17 C-130E Hercules to RAF Mildenhall in the spring of 1988 for their annual ten weeks of temporary duty in Europe. During the deployment three C-130s each were stationed in Greece and Turkey and rotated with those at Mildenhall, where TDY Hercules units are known as 'Bravo Squadron'

Inset Lieutenant Colonel John J Murphy, Commander of the 61st TAS, proudly displays his unit's campaign ribbons

314TH TACTICAL AIRLIFT WING
BRAVO SQUADRON
SCOREBOARD

Departures   Hours   Sorties   Pax   Cargo (tons)

YES WE CAN!
18 MAY 88

Left When the 50th TAS—also from Little Rock AFB, the US Department of Defence's only C-130 training base—was detached to Mildenhall from October to December 1987, Bravo Squadron flew 3658 hours, in 1510 sorties, carried 13,119 passengers and 5827 tons of freight. The 61st TAS's tally to 18 May 1988 can be seen on the 'scoreboard', backed up by the assurance: *Yes we can!*, and they did

Below Morale (and humour) among the Green Hornets runs high. Don't ask us to interpret the 'in' jokes on the crew board. Lieutenant Colonel Murphy says the Jones/Daigle crew are known as The Three Amigos and have Hispanic backgrounds (and a penchant for cartoon characters, it seems), while French/Miller appear to have had some kind of incident . . .

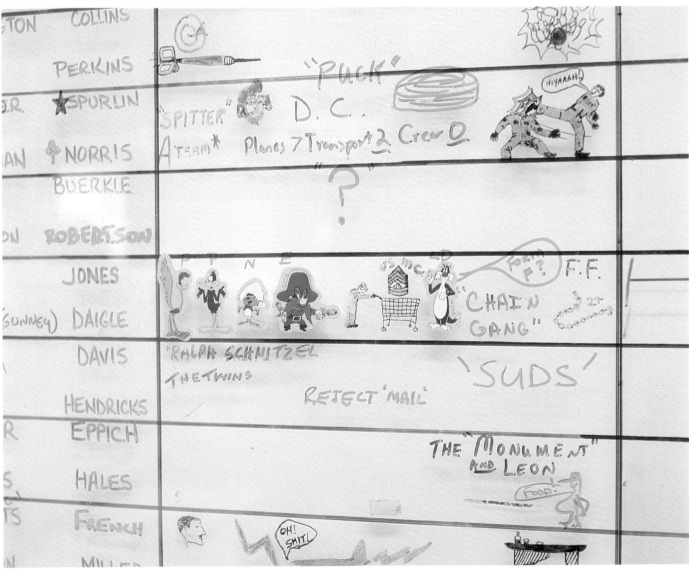

61st TAS C-130E 64-0557 of Bravo
Squadron at the holding point. In
addition to flying low level missions,
often with as many as 44 ships in
trail at 2000 feet, Bravo Squadron
operates the twice weekly European
Eagle scheduled service carrying
up to 64 passengers (including
service families and children) to
destinations in Italy, Spain and West
Germany

In typical 1988 British spring weather C-130E 63-7894 crewed by pilot Captain Steven King and copilot 1st Lieutenant Mike Bumgardner taxies back to the Bravo Squadron ramp behind 63-7769 after a mission. The 61st TAS is involved in many special missions: *Volant Banner* is Presidential support; *Volant Silver*, Vice-Presidential support, while *Volant Pine* (note badge on port lower flight deck window) is a NATO support mission

Heavy Lifters: C-5 and C-141

Is that the aeroplane, or the factory they built it in? The 34,795 cubic feet lower deck cargo hold of a Lockheed C-5B Galaxy is an awesome sight. It can accommodate 36 standard 463L load pallets, but other typical loads can include 16 ¾-ton trucks; two M-1 Abrams tanks or one M-1 and two Bradley armoured fighting vehicles; six McDonnell Douglas AH-64A Apache helicopters; ten Pershing missiles with towing and launching vehicles; or 270 combat-ready troops

Left Pictured with its nose 'visor' up permitting straight-in loading of cargo is C-5B 86-0014 of 301st Military Airlift Squadron (Associate) AFRES, 60th Military Airlift Wing from Travis AFB, California. It arrived at Mildenhall after 12 hours aloft staging Travis-Kirtland AFB, Albuquerque, New Mexico–RAF Fairford, having among its passengers Air Chief Marshal Sir Peter Harding, Air Officer Commander-in-Chief, RAF Strike Command

Right and main picture overleaf C-5A 69-0007 of the 60th MAW awaits unloading on Mildenhall's high security 'hot cargo' area, sited well away from the main ramp and guarded by members of the base's 513th SPS

Right 'Kneeling' facility of the C-5A's main landing gear is well illustrated here, enabling the main deck rear loading ramp to be brought closer to the ground. Seventy-seven of the 81 C-5As delivered to the USAF remain in service, all having been re-winged in a service life extension programme completed in the summer of 1987

Left and overleaf C-5A 70-0464 of the 436th MAW loads up with passengers for a flight to its home base at Dover AFB, Delaware. US Service personnel including their dependents (babies and teddy bears, too) can travel to the USA for $10 in military transports subject to space availability and last-minute diversions. Up to 73 passengers and two loadmasters/flight attendants can be accomodated in rearward-facing seats in the upper deck cabin

C-5B 86-0019 of the 436th MAW displays its high lift devices. The Galaxy's wing spans 222 feet $8\frac{1}{2}$ inches—18 feet shorter than the Soviet Antonov An-124 *Condor*. Fifty C-5Bs are on order for the USAF, and delivery should have been complete by February 1989. The first flight of the -B model took place on 10 September 1985. The C-5A and C-5B are externally similar, the new aircraft incorporating all modifications and improvements progressively introduced on its predecessor

Below Groundcrewman gives scale to the C-5B's massive main landing gear comprising two tandem units per side, each containing a 'triangular footprint' six-wheel bogie, one pair of wheels forward and two pairs aft of the strut. 'High flotation' gear permits operation off unpaved surfaces, with castoring for ground manoeuvring and a 20-degree offset facility for crosswind landings

Left Crew entry door of the behemoth C-5B. *Watch your step* is right; there are an awful lot of them up to the Galaxy's flight deck

Above C-5A 69-0007 on the 'hot cargo' ramp. Smoke in the background is from the engines of a KC-135Q tanker undergoing ground runs

Left Despite its size 'Fat Albert' is no slouch on take-off. Here C-5A 70-0447 of the 436th MAW gets airborne after using little more than half of Mildenhall's 11,000 foot runway. At a maximum gross weight of 837,000 pounds the 'book' figure for take-off ground roll on a standard day is just over a mile and a half. On 17 December 1984 a C-5A set US national records for payload (245,731 pounds) and maximum take-off weight (920,836 pounds). Thought provoker: the Galaxy's maximum *payload* is equivalent to a dozen fully-loaded USAFE C-23A Sherpa light STOL transports

Above and overleaf No, there is nothing wrong with 00447's undercarriage: the main gear bogies rotate through 90 degrees before retracting inwards into the sponson housings

Lockheed's C-141 Starlifter first entered service with Military Airlift Command in April 1965. Between 1979 and 82 270 remaining C-141A models were rebuilt as C-141Bs with a 23 foot 4 inches fuselage stretch made up of two 'plugs' fore and aft of the wing centre section. The added cargo capacity increased MAC's airlift capability by the equivalent of another 90 aircraft. These C-141Bs are from (front to rear): 438th MAW, McGuire AFB, New Jersey; 437th MAW, Charleston AFB, South Carolina, and 63rd MAW, Norton AFB, California

Left A 'K' loader nudges palletized cargo through the clamshell rear loading doors of the 11,399 cubic foot hold of 437th MAW C-141B 65-0266. Starlifters are also used for trooping, paradropping and medevac missions, in which roles they can carry up to 200 combat-equipped troops, 155 paratroops or 103 litter patients respectively

Above White top C-141B 64-0623 of the 438th MAW from McGuire AFB, New Jersey in front of the six-bay freight sheds at Mildenhall's MAC Terminal

Below Fat Albert and son. Huge though it is, this lizard camouflaged C-141B is dwarfed by the 'white top' C-5A behind

Right 64-0623's fin carries the badges of the 438th MAW and its AFRES Associate 514th MAW

Wing walker. Staff Sergeant Ken Doffek of 313th CAMS takes a last look around the wing of a C-141B as dusk falls

Below left The dorsal hump behind the flight deck of this 438th MAW C-141B is a Universal Aerial Refuelling Receptacle Slipway Installation (UARRSI) which enables the Starlifter to be refuelled in flight using either boom or hose-and-drogue methods. The UARRSI was incorporated when C-141As were rebuilt to 'B standard

Above left Men and women of the 313th Consolidated Aircraft Maintenance Squadron fixing an anti-icing bleed air fault on a C-141B of the 437th MAW. The 21,000 lb st thrust Pratt & Whitney TF33-P-7 turbofan was removed from its pylon, lowered to this position, repaired and returned to service within 12 hours, work proceeding through the night in a fine example of 'Team Mildenhall' at work

Below Twin security lights peer through the darkness, giving this C-141B an eerie 'War of the Worlds' aura

Work goes on around the clock to get this 437th MAW Starlifter ready for a homeward bound flight next morning

Naval Air Facility

Mildenhall's Naval Air Facility has three twin-turboprop Beech US-12 liason aircraft on strength. The US Navy operates 73 UC-12s; Bu No 163840 is the latest 1987/88 UC-12M model, Navy equivalent of the Beechcraft Super King Air A200C business aircraft, and is seen here being serviced by Richard Hamrick of Beech Aerospace Services Inc, one of four civilians contracted to maintain the NAF Mildenhall fleet. Powered by a pair of 850 shp Pratt & Whitney Canada PT6A-42 turboprops, the UC-12M flies 30 knots faster and carries 600 pounds more payload than earlier UC-12B models. NAF Commanding Officer Commander 'Hank' Zambie says their job is to get urgent spares and personnel to wherever the US Navy needs them around Europe. His Beechcraft fly 180–200 hours a month, have a 120 nautical mile range and can fly from Mildenhall to Sixth Fleet Headquarters at Naples in four hours

'Just Passing Through'

Elderly US Navy Douglas KA-3B Skywarrior tanker Bu No 147648 was one of two visiting Mildenhall during exercises in the UK. The KA-3B, which can carry 5026 US gallons of fuel—two thirds of which can be offloaded in flight to other aircraft— is on the strength of VAK-308 with Reserve Carrier Air Wing Thirty at NAS Alameda, California

Two Fairchild-Republic A-10A Thunderbolt IIs from the 510th Tactical Fighter Squadron, 81st Tactical Fighter Wing at RAF Bentwaters/Woodbridge, Suffolk, parked on Mildenhall's Base Operations ramp. Pairs or quartets of A-10As are a familiar sight hunting 'Warpac armour' low over the flatlands of East Anglia, where the watchword among civilian fliers is: if you see one Warthog, be sure there's another (or more) close by. The A-10A furthest from camera was flown in by Major General William Kirk James, Commander of the Third Air Force, to which all USAFE units in the United Kingdom are attached

This Lockheed WC-130H Hercules weather reconnaissance aircraft was
pressed into airlift duties with the 403rd Tactical Airlift Wing, AFRES from
Keesler AFB, Mississippi, transporting personnel from the 133 TAW, Air
National Guard at Minneapolis-St Paul International Airport back to USA after
exercises in Europe

Below C-21A Learjet (military version of the Learjet 35A business jet) 84-0081 of 7005th ABS from Stuttgart Airport, West Germany ready to taxi from the Mildenhall Base Ops VIP pick-up point. The USAF operates 78 C-21As in the operational support airlift role from 16 bases in the European, Pacific and United States theatres for time-sensitive movement of cargo and personnel

Above Beech C-12F Operational Support Aircraft 84-0162 of the 58th Military Airlift Squadron from Ramstein AFB, West Germany takes on fuel on Mildenhall's Base Ops ramp. Note four-bladed propellers

Above right Civilian cargo aircraft and airliners on charter to the military are frequent visitors to Mildenhall. Here one of the USAF's stick insect-like 'K' loaders feeds a Southern Air Transport Boeing 707-369C with afterburnerless Pratt & Whitney TF30 turbofans from General Dynamics F-111F strike aircraft for shipment Stateside to be overhauled

SAT's Comtran Super Q 'quietized' Boeing 707 N523SJ rotates for take-off en route to the Oklahoma Air Logistics Center at Tinker AFB, Oklahoma

Boeing E-3B Sentry 76-61605 of 552nd Airborne Warning and Control Wing from Tinker AFB, Oklahoma was one of two AWACS RONing at Mildenhall during exercises over the UK. Two prototypes and 22 production E-3As have been upgraded to E-3B standard with ECM-resistant voice communications suites, additional HF and UHF avionics, Have Quick anti-jamming improvements to UHF radios, a faster IBM CC-2 computer with increased processing speed and greatly expanded memory, five additional situation display consoles (SDCs) and an austere maritime surveillance capability incorporated in the basic radar system

Busy man on Mildenhall's fast turnaround transient ramp is Senior Airman Craig Dubose of 513th Organisational Maintenance Squadron, seen here getting a Shorts C-23A Sherpa started up ready for departure. All C-23As (maximum cruising speed 190 knots) use the call sign POKEY so that Military Air Traffic know they're not exactly dealing with the fastest thing aloft. The USAF ordered 18 of the

busy twin turboprop STOL transports in 1984 to serve as European Distribution System Aircraft (EDSA), ferrying spare parts on a daily scheduled 'round robin' of USAFE bases. Seen here is 84-0471, named *Aviano* after the USAFE base in Italy and captained by 1st Lieutenant Paul Baliker of the 10th Military Airlift Squadron based at Zweibruken, West Germany. When it arrived at Mildenhall the

C-23A had already made stops at USAFE facilities at RAFs Kemble, Upper Heyford, Alconbury and Bentwaters. Currently the only British-built aircraft in the USAF inventory, the Sherpas will be joined by C-29A flight-check versions of the British Aerospace BAe 125-800 business jet during 1988/89